IN THEIR OWN WORDS

SITTING BULL

Peter Roop and Connie Roop

SCHOLASTIC
REFERENCE

For Roger: A gentle leader, an inspiring holy man, a friend.

Copyright © 2002 by Peter Roop and Connie Roop

All rights reserved. Published by Scholastic Inc.

SCHOLASTIC and associated logos are trademarks and/or registered trademarks of Scholastic Inc.

LIBRARY OF CONGRESS CATALOGING-IN-PUBLICATION DATA

Roop, Connie
Sitting Bull/Connie Roop and Peter Roop.
p.   cm.—(In their own words)
Includes bibliographical references and index.
1. Sitting Bull, 1834?–1890—Juvenile literature.   2. Hunkpapa Indians—Biography—Juvenile literature.   3. Dakota Indians—Biography—Juvenile literature.   [1. Sitting Bull, 1834?–1890.   2. Hunkpapa Indians—Biography.   3. Indians of North America—Great Plains—Biography.   4. Dakota Indians—History.]   I. Roop, Peter.   II. Title. III. In their own words (Scholastic)
E99.D1 S613 200
978.004′9752—dc21
[B]   2001020036

ISBN 0-439-26322-0

10 9 8 7 6   05 06

Composition by Brad Walrod
Printed in the U.S.A.
First printing, March 2002

CONTENTS

CHAPTER 1

INTRODUCTION

"A WARRIOR I HAVE BEEN. Now, it is all over. A hard time I have."

Sitting Bull sang this song when he surrendered to the United States government in 1881. It was one of his last songs. Even though his life was hard, it was remarkable.

"I was born on the bank of the Missouri River," Sitting Bull said. He did not tell the year. His people, the Hunkpapa tribe of the Lakota Sioux nation, did not count a man's life by years. Instead, they counted the winters he had lived, laughed, and loved.

Sitting Bull was probably born in 1831, the year the Hunkpapa called "The-Winter-When-

Yellow-Eyes-Played-In-The-Snow." Fifty-nine winters later Sitting Bull—hunter, father, warrior, holy man, friend, and chief—died.

Those fifty-nine winters saw dramatic changes in Lakota life. No longer could the Lakota erect their tipis wherever they wished. No longer did millions of buffalo roam the Plains, providing the Lakota with food, shelter, and clothing. No longer could the Lakota live as a free people.

Those same years saw changes across America. Steamboats churned its rivers. Telegraph wires crisscrossed the countryside. Forests fell to make room for farms and cities. Photography captured images of people and scenes for the first time. The Civil War was fought, and slavery ended. A railroad united the states from "sea to shining sea." Thousands of people came to America to find freedom. State after state joined the Union.

Those changes affected Sitting Bull and all the Lakota people. As long as he could, Sitting Bull fought to keep the Lakota way of life alive.

Sitting Bull lived from about 1831 to 1890. He witnessed many changes to the way of life of his people, the Lakota Sioux.

Sitting Bull's struggle brought him into conflict with the United States government. His success in fighting the government made Sitting Bull a household name all across America.

Like many famous people, Sitting Bull wrote his autobiography, the story of his life. The Lakota, however, did not have a written language. Sitting Bull told some of his adventures in pictures. He recorded his life using crayons on paper. His pictures showed many of his deeds as a warrior. Friends, relatives, and even his enemies also recorded things Sitting Bull did and said.

Sitting Bull had many adventures to share. When a warrior like Sitting Bull did a brave deed, he earned an eagle feather. It might be for killing his first buffalo or for performing bravely in battle. He might earn a feather for being wounded or for stealing horses from an enemy.

Sitting Bull earned more than 100 eagle feathers for his courageous deeds! Never a boastful man, he usually wore only one or two feathers in his hair.

Sitting Bull's drawings are primary sources. A

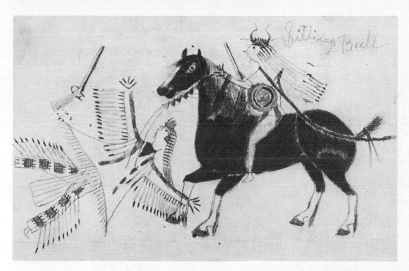

The sketch shows Sitting Bull mounted on a horse and fighting with another Native American. This is just one of many pictographs that Sitting Bull drew to illustrate the events of his life.

primary source is an eyewitness account of an event someone saw or in which he or she participated.

Sitting Bull did not speak English. Many things he said and stories told about him were first spoken in the Lakota and other Native American languages, then translated into English. Those records are primary sources, too. Primary sources help us see or experience events as if we were there ourselves.

A secondary source is a description of a person or

an event by someone who was not there. A biography like this book is a secondary source, although many primary sources were used to research it.

Sitting Bull's words and drawings, the words of people who knew him, newspaper interviews, letters, and photographs were used as primary sources in writing this biography.

Sitting Bull, galloping on horseback, knew the thrill of the buffalo hunt. He faced fierce winter winds and enjoyed gentle breezes. He knew summer heat and bitter winter cold. He thrilled in the danger of stealing horses and facing an enemy. He struggled with hard decisions about his people's welfare. Finally he suffered the defeat of surrender.

Here, through many of his own words and the words of those who knew him, is Sitting Bull's story.

JUMPING BADGER

"WAKANTANKA, FATHER, GREAT Spirit, behold this boy! Your ways he shall see!"

This Lakota prayer was probably sung the day of Sitting Bull's birth into the Hunkpapa tribe of the Lakota nation.

No one knows exactly when Sitting Bull was born. The best guess is 1831. He said, "I was born on the bank of the Missouri River, so I was told by my mother." He was born in present-day South Dakota at a place the Hunkpapa called Many Caches. There they hid food in the many pits—called caches—they had dug.

It was a cold March day when Sitting Bull was born in his family's tipi. Her-Holy-Door, his mother, gently cleaned him. She wrapped him in a soft rabbit skin. His proud father, Returns Again, shared the news of the birth with family and friends.

From his birth, Sitting Bull learned to be Hunkpapa: brave, courageous, generous, and wise.

His parents named him Jumping Badger. Why? No one knows. Maybe he wiggled his legs as if he wanted to jump like a badger and run. Jumping Badger was the first of three names Sitting Bull would have during his life.

Her-Holy-Door pinched his nostrils shut whenever the baby cried. If he cried again, she pinched harder. A Lakota baby must learn to be silent. What if an enemy heard his cry and attacked? A baby's cry could also scare away buffalo during a hunt.

Strapped in his cradleboard, Jumping Badger watched tipi life. He saw his mother cooking and his sister, Good Feather, playing. He watched his father making arrows. He listened to his family talk, tease, and laugh.

That spring Jumping Badger experienced the outside world. He watched the wind ripple the

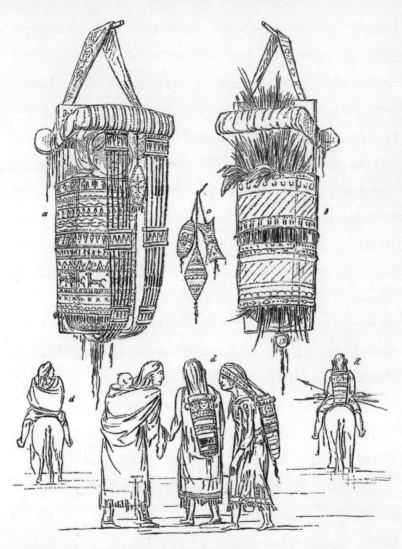

Like other Lakota children, Sitting Bull spent most of the first six months of his life strapped into a cradleboard. His mother carried him around in it during the day, and he slept in it at night.

prairie grass and bend the rainbow of flowers growing up around him. He gazed at ponies grazing.

He watched his aunts cooking, cleaning hides, and carrying water. He saw his uncles caring for ponies, making bows and arrows, and sharing stories. He looked at his cousins racing, playing, swimming, and wrestling.

Life was good for the Hunkpapa. Wakantanka, the Great Spirit, smiled upon the seven Lakota tribes: Hunkpapa, Sans Arc, Miniconjou, Oglala, Brule, Oohenunpa, and Sihasapa.

Jumping Badger, like all Hunkpapa children, was valued and loved. "A child is the greatest gift of Wakantanka," the warrior Higheagle said.

Parents and relatives treated children with gentle humor and great affection. They never spanked a child. A stern look was warning enough.

Jumping Badger's parents noticed how he stared at things for a long time. He looked at the fire or gazed at the smoke hole at the top of the tipi. He studied his food before eating. His intense eyes followed his family everywhere.

As he outgrew his cradleboard, Jumping Badger crawled around the tipi. He felt the thick buffalo sleeping robes. He touched his father's favorite bow. He studied each object deliberately and slowly.

One time he crawled toward the cooking fire. He was curious about the flickering flames. Her-Holy-Door watched him. The Lakota say, "One must learn from the bite of the fire to let it alone."

Jumping Badger passed his tiny hand through the flames. Without a cry he yanked it back. He stared at his hurting hand, then at the burning fire. Jumping Badger now knew the pain of a burn.

As he grew, Jumping Badger explored and examined his world. He ran to see his uncles Four Horns and Looks-for-Him-in-a-Tent. He dashed to help his father tend their ponies. He sprinted to swim with friends or to chase them.

A curious boy, Jumping Badger studied everything. He held a grasshopper all morning and watched an eagle soar all afternoon. He gazed at swimming fish and stared at tadpoles.

Jumping Badger was so slow and deliberate he was

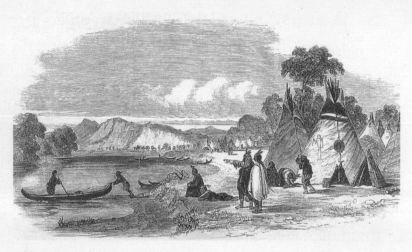

This picture shows a Sioux encampment along the upper Missouri River during Sitting Bull's time.

nicknamed Hunkesni, or Slow. This did not mean he was not smart. Slow was a loving name. It meant he thought before he acted.

All his life Slow remained thoughtful, looking before he leapt into action.

Slow was this unusual boy's second name. Later he earned the name by which he is best known, Sitting Bull.

SLOW

HUNKPAPA CHILDREN DID NOT go to a formal school. The world around them was their school. Their parents and relatives taught them the skills they needed to survive.

Slow moved around the circle of tipis listening and learning. Later he said, "In my early days, I was eager to learn and do things, and therefore I learned quickly."

Slow's family lived in a small band called a *tiyopaye*. Most people in Slow's *tiyopaye* were relatives. Slow's band was called Icihaha. Icihaha means "Those Who Laugh at Each Other."

Slow called his father's cousins, uncles, and

brothers "Father." They would be like fathers to him as he grew up.

Growing up as a Hunkpapa was not easy. A Hunkpapa man had to be a good hunter to provide his family's food. He had to have courage in battle and be able to sneak into an enemy camp to steal horses. He must be kind. He must endure pain, cold, and sickness and face death without fear.

Slow spent days with his many fathers tracking deer, antelope, and elk. He learned how to tell when an enemy passed. He practiced with his bow and arrows.

Slow's first bow was small, his arrows blunt. As he grew stronger, he was given a man's bow with sharp arrows.

Slow learned how to ride almost as soon as he could walk. Horses were the key to survival on the Plains. They carried warriors into battle. Hunters on horseback chased buffalo. Horses pulled travois—wooden poles loaded with the family's tipi—when the band moved camp.

When he was three years old, Slow could climb

Many Native Americans that lived on the Plains used a travois to transport their belongings from one place to another. The travois did not have any wheels. Instead, the ends of the poles dragged along the ground.

up a horse's leg, onto its back, and ride. When he was five, he was given his own horse. He tenderly cared for it. Lakota fathers told their boys, "Son, it is cowardly to be cruel. Be good to your pony."

Slow was placed in charge of his family's horse herd when he was seven. He groomed them, tended their injuries, and rode them.

Slow enjoyed skills of strength. He competed with his friends Bear's Rib, Red Feather, Thunder Hawk, Crawler, and Circling Hawk.

Slow practiced running until he was the fastest boy in the band. He swam until he was the best. He practiced shooting arrows until he could shoot them through a rolling hoop without missing. He galloped on horseback so he could be first in battle.

Slow thrilled at playing the "Hoop Game." Using sticks, boys tried to roll a wooden hoop into the opposing team's goal. Battling to win, the boys smashed hard into one another.

Slow especially enjoyed the game "Throwing Them Off Their Horses." In this game, players knocked one another off galloping horses. If a boy fell, he might break an arm or be knocked out. Even injured, a boy must keep playing to show his bravery.

Slow did not brag when he won. He took his prizes of knives and arrows modestly. Once he won ten buffalo skins, but he did not tease the loser. When he lost a game, Slow accepted the loss as a good sport.

One day soon Slow's father would ask him to go on a buffalo hunt. Slow longed for the day to come. The shaggy buffalo gave the Lakota tribes everything they needed. Buffalo meat was eaten fresh and dried for winter. Skins were tanned into soft leather for leggings, shirts, skirts, and tipis. Hollow horns became cups and spoons. Bones were shaped into digging tools. Bladders made pouches; hooves made glue. Skulls were saved for ceremonies.

The Hunkpapa could not survive without buffalo. Each year they needed to hunt thousands to keep the tribe healthy.

When he killed his first buffalo, Slow would no longer be a boy. He would be a Hunkpapa youth. Maybe he could even change his name.

BUFFALO HUNTER

MANY LAKOTA CHANGED THEIR names during their lifetimes. Often it was to honor a brave deed or an event.

Slow's father, Returns Again, gained his name because of his bravery. In battle he would attack, retreat, and "return again" to fight.

Returns Again changed his name again when Slow was a boy. He was hunting with three friends when they heard a strange rumbling noise. It was a huge buffalo! The other hunters wanted to kill the buffalo. Returns Again said no, he was listening to the animal.

The buffalo said, *"Tatan'ka Iyota'ke. Tatan'ka Psi'ca. Tatan'ka winyuha Najin'. Tatan'ka Wanji'la."*

Then, with a shake of its head, the buffalo ran away.

The buffalo had spoken of the four stages of life: childhood, youth, maturity, old age. "Sitting Bull. Jumping Bull. Bull-Standing-With-Cow. Lone Bull." Each name stood for a time in a man's life.

To honor the buffalo, Returns Again changed his name to Sitting Bull, the first name the buffalo had spoken.

One spring day in 1841 Hunkpapa scouts rode into camp. Word spread that a herd of buffalo grazed nearby. The men prepared for the hunt.

Sitting Bull invited ten-year-old Slow to join them. The day Slow had dreamed of had arrived. He mounted his horse and followed his father.

When they saw the buffalo, the hunters surrounded the herd. Sitting Bull told Slow to pick a calf. Slow carefully studied the herd before selecting a young buffalo. Slow wanted to ride ahead, but he waited patiently.

Native Americans who lived on the Plains depended on buffalo for food and clothing. Because buffalo were so important, boys learned to hunt them at a very young age.

When the chief hunter shouted, "*Hopo! Hopo!*" "Go! Go!" the men raced at the herd.

Slow pressed his knees against his pony's sides, guiding it toward the calf he had chosen. He carefully aimed an arrow and killed the young buffalo.

He had made his first kill!

Over time, Slow shot many more buffalo calves and became known as a generous hunter. By sharing his kills with poor people, he showed his generous nature. All his life, Slow shared with those who had little.

"When I was ten years old, I was famous as a hunter," Sitting Bull said. "My speciality was buffalo calves. I gave the calves that I killed to the poor who had no horses. I was considered a good man."

Before a hunt Slow sang this hunting song:

> *I go to kill the buffalo*
> *Wakantanka sent the buffalo*
> *On hills, in plains and woods.*
> *So give me my bow; give me my bow;*
> *I go to kill the buffalo.*

After a successful hunt, Slow sang, "Grandfather [the buffalo], my children are hungry. You were created for that. So I must kill you."

After his first buffalo kill, Slow became a young man. He did not, however, change his name. Now he must face the next major step in growing up. He must prove himself as a warrior.

SITTING BULL

BECOMING A WARRIOR WAS ONE OF Slow's goals. Warriors were respected. They became leaders. Warriors stole the enemy's horses and grew rich. Giving horses away would be another way Slow could show his generosity.

Slow was eager to ride on raids to steal horses, especially against the Crow, a longtime Hunkpapa enemy.

Slow dreamed of touching an enemy, the bravest deed of all. It was called "counting coup." Most warriors carried a coup stick, which they used to touch the enemy. Coups were also counted if a warrior used a lance or a bow. Any warrior could shoot an arrow at an enemy. Only the bravest warriors dared to ride close enough to an enemy to touch him and count coup.

One day, when Slow was about fourteen, he had his chance to ride on a raid.

The Icihaha band was camped near Crow hunting lands.

Good Voiced Elk, a leading warrior, said he was going to fight the Crow. He would steal horses. He invited others to join him.

Slow's father, Sitting Bull, and ten warriors rode with Good Voiced Elk.

Slow decided to follow them. He did not ride too fast, however. If the warriors saw him, they would tell him to go home.

Later, Slow and his horse caught up with the men. He said, "We are going, too."

Slow's father was unhappy. Seeing Slow's eagerness, though, Good Voiced Elk let him join.

Sitting Bull gave Slow his coup stick saying, "You have a good running horse. Try to do something brave."

Slow would not disgrace his father. A Lakota man

often told his son, "I never want to see you live to be an old man. Die young on the battlefield. That is the way a Lakota dies." The Lakota believed a true warrior did not die in old age.

On the fourth morning the Lakota saw twelve Crow warriors. They prepared to fight by applying war paint.

Every man watched and waited for Good Voiced Elk to give the signal to attack.

Slow, eager for his first fight, wiggled on his horse.

The Crow rode closer.

Slow, who had always been patient, could no longer wait. Suddenly, he kicked his horse, yelled a war cry, and galloped toward the surprised Crow.

The other Lakota rode after him.

The Crow galloped away. One Crow warrior, however, jumped off his horse and faced Slow.

Slow raced straight at him, determined to count coup or die. The Crow aimed an arrow at Slow. Before he could shoot, Slow hit him with his coup stick.

"*On-hey!*" Slow shouted. "I, Slow, have conquered him!"

This picture drawn by Sitting Bull shows him counting coup. To count coup, a young man showed his bravery in battle by touching the enemy with a coup stick.

Slow had counted his first coup!

Good Voiced Elk's raiding party rode back to their village with many Crow horses. They were welcomed with shouts of joy.

Slow's family held a feast in his honor. Sitting Bull proudly placed an eagle feather in Slow's hair to show he had counted his first coup.

As another honor, Sitting Bull gave away many of his horses to the poor.

Sitting Bull then painted Slow black from head to

toe. Black was the Lakota color for victory. He gave Slow a new horse. Sitting Bull proudly led his son around a circle of tipis. Over and over Sitting Bull shouted, "My son has struck the enemy! He is brave!"

Then came the moment Slow had hoped for. He received a new name.

His father gave Slow his own name, Sitting Bull. "I call him Takan'ka Iyota'ke! Sitting Bull."

The boy, Slow, was gone. The man, Sitting Bull, had come.

He would be called Sitting Bull until the end of his days. His father took the second name given by the buffalo. He was now Jumping Bull, the proud father of a warrior son.

WARRIOR

THE BEST WARRIORS JOINED GROUPS called *akicitas*. A warrior had to be invited to join an *akicita*. These groups did many jobs within the tribe. One *akicita* led the band when it moved camp, protecting people from enemy attacks.

Other *akicitas* oversaw buffalo hunts. They made sure no overeager hunter scared away the buffalo.

Sitting Bull was invited to join the Strong Heart *akicita*. Becoming a Strong Heart was a great accomplishment. This *akicita* was for the bravest of warriors.

Sitting Bull also helped form an *akicita* called the Midnight Strong Heart Society. These fearless warriors met at midnight to feast, talk, and plan raids.

The shield and lance were the warrior's symbols. Sitting Bull received his first shield from his father. It was decorated with four eagle feathers, one for each direction. It was painted blue, green, red, and brown with a figure of a bird in the center. Sitting Bull carried his shield proudly.

Sitting Bull's father also gave him a wooden lance. It was seven feet long and tipped with an iron point. His mother decorated it with white and blue beads. An eagle feather hung from the end. Sitting Bull kept it in a buffalo-skin case.

When Sitting Bull was young, the Hunkpapa had few guns. Most were old muskets they got from traders. Bullets and gunpowder were scarce. The Hunkpapa could not afford to waste bullets and powder, so they rarely practiced with guns. They saved the precious bullets and powder for hunting and fighting.

Hunkpapa warriors fought only when they wanted to. No one could order a man to fight. Each man made his own decisions. If he liked the warrior leading a war party, he joined him.

The Hunkpapa and other Lakota tribes did not fight as a united team. Battle was a time for a warrior to earn honors by counting coup. He rode into a fight as a member of a war party. When the fighting began, however, he fought alone. He rode fast, counted coup, and galloped away.

For his first coup, Sitting Bull received a white eagle feather. In 1846, when he was fifteen, he earned his first red feather for being wounded in battle. (Red, which the Lakota call *sha*, is a sacred color.)

Sitting Bull earned his *sha* feather in a fight against the Flathead. A group of Hunkpapa had followed buffalo into Flathead territory north of the Missouri River.

Scouts spotted Flathead warriors nearby, and a raiding party was organized. Sitting Bull eagerly joined.

Twenty Flathead warriors charged the Hunkpapa. Both sides fired arrows and bullets, and then the Flathead made a battle line.

Sitting Bull shouted that he would ride in front of the enemy, letting them shoot at him. This was called "Riding the Daring Line" and displayed a warrior's bravery.

Galloping at full speed, Sitting Bull rode the daring line. His friends shouted encouragement. Bullets and arrows whizzed by. When he reached the end of the line, however, a bullet struck his foot. He proudly rode back to his cheering friends. Luckily, the foot wound was not serious.

For this brave deed, Sitting Bull received his first red feather. Later in life he earned more red feathers for wounds to his arm and hip.

His worst wound came in a fight with a Crow warrior. When Sitting Bull was twenty-five winters old, he went on a raid to steal horses from a Crow camp. As he was escaping, Sitting Bull came face-to-face with one of the enemy.

Armed with an old rifle, Sitting Bull fired and hit the Crow warrior. Before dying, the Crow shot Sitting Bull in his left foot.

A medicine man cared for his wound, but it never

Sitting Bull was a modest man. Although he received dozens of feathers for acts of bravery in battle, he usually wore only a single eagle feather.

healed properly. For the rest of his life, Sitting Bull walked with a limp. Still determined to be the best, Sitting Bull practiced until he could run almost as fast as he did before.

Sitting Bull became well known to enemy tribes as a fierce warrior. Sometimes his friends would shout, "Sitting Bull, I am he!" or "We are Sitting Bull's boys!" to strike fear into enemies of the Hunkpapa.

In 1857, Sitting Bull saved an enemy boy's life. Sitting Bull and his men had chased a group of Assiniboine across a shallow lake. Sitting Bull counted two coups.

Swift Cloud, a Hunkpapa warrior, chased a thirteen-year-old boy. The boy fought hard, but Swift Cloud captured him. He was going to kill him when Sitting Bull ran up.

The boy sensed something powerful about Sitting Bull. He threw his arms around him, crying, "Older Brother!"

Sitting Bull asked Swift Cloud to spare the boy and to give the boy to him. Swift Cloud argued, but

Sitting Bull won. Later, Sitting Bull adopted the boy as his younger brother.

In 1859, Sitting Bull's father was killed in battle. The Hunkpapa were fighting Crow warriors. Jumping Bull was suffering from a horrible toothache. His jaw hurt so much he wanted to die. The battle gave him his chance to end his pain and show his bravery.

Jumping Bull attacked a Crow warrior, shouting, "Leave him to me!"

Jumping Bull reached for his knife, but it had slid behind his back. The Crow stabbed Jumping Bull to death.

Sitting Bull then killed the Crow with his lance.

That night some captured Crow children and women were going to be put to death to avenge Jumping Bull.

Sitting Bull took pity and said, "If you intend to do this for my sake, take good care of them and let them live. My father is a man, and death is his."

Sitting Bull gave his father's name to his adopted brother, the boy he had saved. Jumping Bull remained a loyal brother all of his life.

HOLY MAN

ANOTHER IMPORTANT PART OF Sitting Bull's life was his relationship with Wakantanka, the Great Spirit. Like every Lakota boy, Sitting Bull went on a vision quest. During a vision quest a boy did not eat or sleep until Wakantanka had spoken to him. This could take days.

History does not tell us how old Sitting Bull was when he went on his vision quest. Most likely, it was before counting his first coup.

Sitting Bull was well prepared for his vision quest. His most important teachers were his father, mother, and uncle Four Horns. They taught him to see *wakan*, the spirit, in everything, especially in the buffalo and the eagle.

When Sitting Bull was ready, he went to the *Wichasha Wakan*, a holy man. The vision quest was a private matter between Sitting Bull and his *Wichasha Wakan*.

Sitting Bull then went into the sweat lodge. Water was poured on hot rocks, so the steam could purify Sitting Bull. The steam cleansed his heart, mind, body, and spirit. Then, without food or water, Sitting Bull climbed to a hilltop.

Sitting Bull waited for Wakantanka to send a vision. He stayed there alone until his vision appeared. Hungry and weak he returned to his village. His family gave a feast in his honor.

Afterward, Sitting Bull shared his vision with the *Wichasha Wakan*. The holy man told Sitting Bull his vision's meaning. Together, they kept his vision a secret.

Sitting Bull's vision must have been powerful. He spent the rest of his life mastering the skills of a holy man. He also learned the healing arts and carried healing medicines with him.

Sitting Bull became a well-known singer as well.

In addition to being a brave hunter and warrior, Sitting Bull enjoyed drawing sketches and singing.

The Lakota say, "Let me make the songs of a nation, and I do not care who makes its laws."

Sitting Bull made battle songs and hunting songs. He created songs for the dead. Many of his songs were about animals. Sitting Bull enjoyed singing like his bird friends, especially the meadowlark and bobolink.

Sitting Bull was friendly to wolves, too. Once he found a wolf wounded by two arrows. The wolf said, "Boy, if you relieve me, your name shall be great."

Sitting Bull pulled out the arrows and used his medicines to heal the wounds.

He created a wolf song:

> *Alone in the wilderness I roam.*
> *With much hardships*
> *In the wilderness I roam.*
> *A wolf said this to me.*

The wolf was right. Sitting Bull's name would become great among his people and beyond.

Sitting Bull showed his people how a Lakota man should live. He fed the elderly and gave horses to the poor. He was brave in battle. He showed mercy. He was kind, especially to children. All his life, Sitting Bull gave gifts to his young friends.

The most important Lakota ceremony of the year was the Sun Dance gathering, which celebrated the Lakota being part of the universe. The dance itself honored Wakantanka, the Great Spirit. The Sun Dance was performed to thank Wakantanka for the things he had given the Lakota the year before.

Lakota traveled great distances for the Sun Dance. They came to see old friends and make new ones. Many relatives saw one another only once a year at the Sun Dance. Here young men and women from different bands met and often married. The Sun Dance feasting and dancing lasted twelve days.

During a Sun Dance, men fulfilled promises to Wakantanka. Sitting Bull danced his first Sun Dance when he was twenty-five winters old. This would have been in June 1856.

To prove his bravery and gain honor, Sitting Bull chose Piercing the Heart Dance for his first Sun Dance. This was the most difficult of all.

Sitting Bull had sticks pushed through his skin, both on his front and back, to show he could

Poles like this one often stood in the middle of the Sun Dance area.

withstand great pain for his people. Staring at the
sun, he danced and sang. He prayed to Wakantanka
to give his people food and good health.

While dancing, Sitting Bull heard a voice say,
"Wakantanka gives you what you ask for. Wakantanka
will grant your wish."

Sitting Bull danced many Sun Dances during his
life. One of his adopted sons, One Bull, said, "Sitting
Bull danced often. He wanted to learn to love his
god and his people."

From his first vision to the end of his days, Sitting Bull prayed and sacrificed for the good of his people.

The more the Americans trespassed into the Lakota world, the more Sitting Bull's skills as a hunter, warrior, leader, and holy man would be needed.

HUSBAND AND FATHER

SITTING BULL MARRIED FIVE TIMES during his life. Lakota men often married more than once. Life was dangerous on the Plains. Many men died in battle, in accidents, or while hunting. Many women were left without husbands. Children were without fathers. In some bands, there were three women for every man.

To provide food and to protect widows and orphans, Lakota men were allowed more than one wife. Many girls wanted to marry Sitting Bull because he was a great hunter and brave warrior.

Sitting Bull first married when he was twenty winters old. He fell in love with Light Hair, a girl from his band. Light Hair and Sitting Bull often talked standing up, wrapped in a buffalo robe. This was how the couple dated. To marry Light Hair, Sitting Bull gave her father many ponies.

After they were married, Sitting Bull and Light Hair went on a hunting trip. They set up their tipi beneath a tall cottonwood tree along a river.

Sitting Bull killed two buffalo, and the couple loaded the skins and meat on a horse. In camp they worked as a team slicing the meat into thin strips, which they hung on a pole to dry. Dried meat would last many months and was easy to carry.

One night Light Hair was inside the tipi cooking buffalo meat. She cracked open buffalo bones to get out the rich, nourishing fat inside. A pot of shiny fat bubbled over the fire.

Using a horn spoon, Light Hair skimmed off the fat. Looking into the spoon, she saw a scary sight. Through the smoke hole at the top of the tipi, a Crow warrior was reflected in the fat!

Calmly, Light Hair whispered to Sitting Bull, "An enemy is spying on us from above. Do something at once before he takes a shot at us."

The open space at the top of a tipi is called a smoke hole. Smoke from cooking fires was released through this hole.

Sitting Bull took an arrow in one hand. With the other hand he grabbed his bow. Without looking up, he fired the arrow up through the smoke hole.

Sitting Bull leapt outside through the tipi door.

He heard the enemy and lunged after him, but he tripped in the darkness. The Crow warrior escaped.

Holding up a flaming stick, Sitting Bull saw bloody footprints. He had wounded the Crow. There was no way, however, to tell if the enemy still lurked nearby.

"We broke camp at once and returned home," Sitting Bull later said.

Light Hair and Sitting Bull had one son. Unfortunately, Light Hair died giving birth. Sitting Bull was sad about Light Hair's death. But he was proud he had a son who would grow up Lakota.

Sadly, when the boy was only four years old, he got sick and died.

Sitting Bull was alone now. He missed his wife and son. His sister, Good Feather, was married and had two boys. One of the boys, One Bull, was four years old. With Good Feather's blessing, Sitting Bull adopted One Bull as his son. Sitting Bull raised One Bull to be a warrior. Sitting Bull and One Bull hunted and fought together for the rest of their lives.

Sitting Bull married two wives next, Red Woman and Snow-on-Her.

Sadly, the two women did not get along, so Sitting Bull and Snow-on-Her ended their marriage. In 1871, Red Woman died from an illness. Sitting Bull grew lonely. He liked to have family near him, so he married Four Robes. Four Robes had an older sister named Seen-by-the-Nation. Her husband had died and she had two sons, Little Soldier and Blue Mountain, to care for. Four Robes convinced Sitting Bull to marry her sister, too. Sitting Bull adopted the boys as his own.

The tipi quickly grew crowded. Four Robes gave birth to twin boys in 1876. In 1878, a daughter named Standing Holy was born. In 1880, another set of twin boys was born.

When her husband, Jumping Bull, died, Sitting Bull's mother moved into Sitting Bull's tipi, too.

She was concerned for her son and his growing family. She warned him, "You must hang back in war time. You must be careful how you act in war."

Sitting Bull understood. He would not take the risks he had taken when he was younger. His family needed him. Still, he would fight his enemies, the

Crow, Pawnee, Flathead, and American soldiers—especially the American soldiers.

As years passed, Americans came to the Lakota lands. Sitting Bull had little contact with them. He felt that if he left the white people alone, they would leave him alone.

This was not to be.

WAR CHIEF

SITTING BULL KNEW LITTLE OF THE American Civil War, which ended in 1865. It had been fought far to the east of his Hunkpapa homeland.

Hundreds of thousands of soldiers fought in the war. When it ended, some soldiers stayed in the army. The United States government sent these soldiers west to protect American pioneers from Native Americans.

For many years fighting had taken place between other Lakota tribes and Americans crossing their lands. To stop the fighting, the government offered to buy Native American land. U.S. officials believed that if the tribes sold some land, then both sides could live peacefully.

Many treaties between the Native Americans and the United States had been signed before. There was one major misunderstanding about the treaties. When a chief signed the treaty, he signed only for himself. He could ask his people to stop fighting, but each warrior decided what to do for himself.

The Americans, on the other hand, believed a chief represented all his people. They thought the tribe must do what the chief said.

There were other problems, too. The United States government offered to pay for the land with food and supplies. Many times, however, the meat was rotten and the flour spoiled.

Because of these problems and misunderstandings, battles between Americans and Native Americans continued.

As the Native Americans lost battles to the better-armed American soldiers, many surrendered and moved to places called reservations. The United States government set up reservations where the Native Americans were forced to live like white people. They built homes, farmed, and sent their children to school. They received food and supplies at agencies on the reservations. Reservation life was difficult for most Native Americans. They had always been free to live and hunt where they wanted.

When asked to move onto a reservation, Sitting Bull said he would "rather die on the field of battle."

Until the mid-1860s Americans crossing the country were not a problem for Sitting Bull. The trails were too far south to impact the Hunkpapa living north near the Missouri and Yellowstone Rivers.

When the Civil War ended, however, more Americans came up the Missouri River on steamboats. More wagon trains crossed Hunkpapa lands.

For three years, Sitting Bull and other warriors attacked wagon trains, soldiers, and settlers. They felt this was necessary to protect their families and their way of life.

When asked by the government to make peace, Sitting Bull said, "I have killed, robbed, and injured too many white men to believe in a good peace."

The American government wanted to end the

The Oregon Trail opened in 1841 and stretched from Missouri to the Oregon Territory. Thousands of settlers in wagon trains traveled its route across the Plains to find land and jobs.

fighting. The Native American war cost millions of dollars. In 1867, a Catholic priest named Father Pierre Jean De Smet went to talk with the Native Americans. The Native Americans knew Father De Smet and trusted him.

If they signed a new treaty, Father De Smet told them, Americans and Native Americans could live in peace.

The Treaty of 1868 listed rules for who could use land in what is today North Dakota, South Dakota, Montana, Wyoming, and Nebraska. It stated, "No white person or persons shall be permitted to settle upon or occupy any portion [of this land] without the consent of the Indians." White travelers needed permission from the Native Americans to cross reservation land. The hated American military forts would be closed. The Lakota could hunt as long as buffalo were plentiful.

Especially important to the Lakota was that they could keep Paha Sapa, the sacred Black Hills. These tree-covered mountains are in western South Dakota. The Black Hills would belong to the Lakota forever. If any white people entered the Black Hills, the government promised to make them leave.

In return the United States government wanted the Native Americans to stop fighting and live on what was called the Great Sioux Reservation.

Father De Smet came to Sitting Bull's camp to discuss the new treaty. Sitting Bull told him, "I will listen to thy good words, and as bad as I have been to the whites, just as good am I ready to become toward them."

The next day Sitting Bull and his fellow chiefs met with Father De Smet. Ten tipis were set up to make a big lodge for the council. Five hundred warriors surrounded the meeting place.

Father De Smet kept notes of the meeting. He wrote, "The council was opened with songs and dances, noisy, joyful and very wild."

The peace pipe was lit and offered to the sky, Mother Earth, and the four directions.

Father De Smet said, "Your Grandfather [President Andrew Johnson] wishes you to live among your people on your own lands. You will never starve. You will always have plenty of rations. You will not be captives, but at liberty. You will receive warm clothing. . . . End this cruel and unfortunate bloodshed . . . bury all your bitterness toward the whites, forget the past, and accept the hand of peace which is extended to you."

Black Moon, a Lakota chief, told Father De Smet his words were "good and full of truth and meaning."

He said, "But there are many thorns in our hearts, many wounds to heal. We have been cruelly treated and often treacherously deceived." Black Moon finished his speech saying, "Let the past be forgotten."

Later Sitting Bull spoke. He made it clear that he did not want to sign the treaty. He said, "I wish all to know that I do not propose to sell any part of my country, nor will I have the whites cutting our timber along the rivers."

Sitting Bull added, "One more thing. Those forts with white soldiers must be abandoned. There is no greater source of trouble and grievance to my people."

In his notes, Father De Smet wrote that Sitting Bull "sat down amid the cheers of young and old."

Despite Sitting Bull's concerns, two-thirds of the Lakota agreed to the treaty and moved onto the Great Sioux Reservation. Later many more chiefs also signed the Treaty of 1868.

However, Sitting Bull and his followers still refused to sign. They would hunt and live where

Throughout the West, reservation agencies distributed food, clothing, and other rations to Native Americans. Often, however, the supplies never arrived or the food was spoiled.

they pleased. If the whites bothered them, they would fight. If they were left alone, they would leave the whites alone. Sitting Bull said, "Even a bird will defend its nest." The land was his nest. He would defend it.

Other Native Americans agreed with Sitting Bull. They were led by Sitting Bull's uncle Four Horns. They planned to unite to fight the

Americans. As small scattered bands they could not stop the soldiers. Combined, though, they would have enough warriors to drive the whites from the Native Americans' beloved lands.

Four Horns asked the bands to meet in June 1869 for a Sun Dance. Then the grass would be tall, the buffalo plentiful, and the ponies fat.

Bands of Hunkpapa, Oglala, Miniconjou, Sans Arc, Yanktonai, Two Kettles, and Blackfeet tribes set up their tipis along the Rosebud Creek in present-day Montana. These groups had not signed the hated treaty. Bands of Cheyenne and Arapaho who were against the treaty joined them, too.

At the gathering, Four Horns revealed more of his plan. He believed the bands needed to select one leader and unite behind him. This chief would lead them against the Americans. Everyone quickly agreed upon who should be chief. Their choice was Sitting Bull.

In a special ceremony, four important chiefs carried Sitting Bull on a buffalo robe.

Four Horns said, "Because of your bravery on the

This is one of the few photographs where Sitting Bull is shown wearing his many-feathered war bonnet.

battlefields and as the greatest warrior of our bands, we have elected you as our war chief, leader of the entire Lakota nation. When you tell us to fight, we shall fight, when you tell us to make peace, we shall make peace."

Black Moon added, "First, you are to think always of Wakantanka. Second, you are to use all your powers to care for your people, and especially the poor."

To help Sitting Bull, the Oglala warrior Crazy Horse was chosen second in command.

Sitting Bull received a white horse, a new war bonnet, rifle, and a bow and arrows. He sang a special song as he rode through camp:

> Ye tribes, behold me.
> The chiefs of old are gone.
> Myself, I take courage.

Sitting Bull, now chief among chiefs, would guide his people as they fought to keep their Lakota ways.

CHAPTER 10

WAR!

IN 1871, SITTING BULL TURNED forty winters old. He could still fight as well as most warriors, but he now had the future of his people to think about.

Sitting Bull's respected uncle Four Horns told him, "Be a little against fighting, but when anyone shoots, be ready to fight." He wanted his nephew to be more careful now that he was the Lakota's most important leader.

Sitting Bull's first problem as chief arose when the Americans decided to build a railroad from Minnesota to the Washington Territory.

In 1871, the Americans came to Lakota lands looking for the best place for a railroad. The best route ran through the territory surrounding the Yellowstone River. This was a favorite Native American hunting ground. It was also an area the Americans had promised to stay out of according to the Treaty of 1868.

Sitting Bull told his warriors, "If they come shooting, shoot back." He warned them, however, not to shoot first. His warning would not be heeded.

Spotted Eagle, another Lakota chief, joined Sitting Bull's camp in the summer of 1872. There were more than 2,000 families and 1,000 armed warriors there. Spotted Eagle said he "would fight the railroad people as long as he lived."

The Native Americans learned that white soldiers and railroad people were near. Some young warriors, eager to count coup, slipped away from camp to attack the Americans.

Sitting Bull and Crazy Horse rode to help their young men. The American soldiers made a long line. The Lakota warriors charged them, then fell back. The Americans fired again and again, but most of their bullets missed.

The battle was at a standstill. It was then that

Sitting Bull demonstrated his bravery for both sides to see.

Taking his pipe, he calmly walked between the Native Americans and the American soldiers. He shouted in Lakota, "Who other Indians wish to smoke with me come." He sat down and smoked.

Four friends joined him. The men passed the pipe as bullets hit close, shooting up spurts of dust. The warriors kept smoking.

When they finished, Sitting Bull cleaned his pipe, put in it his pouch, and walked back to his side.

Sitting Bull yelled to his men, "That's enough. We must quit, that's enough."

The Native Americans stopped fighting, except Crazy Horse and White Bull. Together, the two men "Rode the Daring Line." Bullets buzzed like angry hornets. One bullet killed Crazy Horse's horse, but Crazy Horse was able to sprint to safety unhurt.

Neither side won the battle. But the Native Americans, under Sitting Bull's leadership, had shown the Americans they would fight.

Later, White Bull, Sitting Bull's nephew, said

smoking the pipe in front of the enemy was "the bravest deed possible."

In March 1873, the United States government decided that the railroad would cross the country, whether the Native Americans liked it or not.

General William Sherman told Congress, "This railroad is a national enterprise. We are forced to protect the men...through, probably, the most warlike nation of Indians [the Lakota] on this continent, who will fight for every foot of the line." Sherman knew he needed to send more soldiers west to protect the people building the railroad.

By midsummer the railroad reached the east side of the Missouri River in what is today North Dakota. On the west side, the army built Fort Abraham Lincoln to house the soldiers in the West.

Lieutenant Colonel George Armstrong Custer commanded the soldiers. Custer was a very popular officer. He had gained glory in the Civil War. Because Custer wore his hair long, the Lakota called him Pehin Hanska, Long Hair.

When George A. Custer graduated from the United States Military Academy, he was at the bottom of his class. However, he went on to gain military fame in the Civil War and in battles against Native Americans in the West.

When Custer learned Sitting Bull's people were near the Yellowstone River, he rode after them. Sitting Bull made sure the women and children in his camp were protected. Then he turned his attention toward Custer. When Custer approached, Sitting Bull's warriors made their escape. They crossed the Yellowstone River in round buffalo-skin boats. Custer had no boats, so the warriors were safe.

The next morning, Sitting Bull's warriors fired at Custer's soldiers across the river. The soldiers fired back, but neither side did much damage.

That afternoon, Sitting Bull's warriors crossed the river to attack the American soldiers. Still, neither side could win. When the soldiers brought out their cannon, the battle ended. Sitting Bull pulled back. So did Custer.

Sitting Bull sang:

> *Young men, help me, do help me!*
> *I love my country so;*
> *That is why I am fighting.*

Fortunately for the Lakota, the railroad ran out of money. Building stopped. An uneasy peace settled over the land.

It did not last long.

The Treaty of 1868 did not allow Americans in the Black Hills. Despite this, Custer led an expedition there in 1874. His goal was to find a place to build a fort even though a fort was also prohibited by the treaty. Custer claimed the fort would protect the Native Americans.

Gold miners rode with Custer. They wanted to see if there was gold in the Black Hills. President Ulysses S. Grant believed that if Americans had more gold to spend, everyone would be better off. Everyone, that is, except the Native Americans.

Custer spent two months in the Black Hills. This upset Sitting Bull. He said, "We have plenty of game. We want no white men here. The Black Hills belong to me. If the whites try to take them, I will fight."

On July 27, 1874, a miner spotted yellow rocks. Gold! Custer wrote to General Philip Sheridan, "I have upon my table forty or fifty particles [pieces] of pure gold."

Custer sent a rider to Fort Lincoln with news. The miners had found gold in the Black Hills! Newspaper headlines across America declared, "EASY MONEY!" and "STIRRING NEWS FROM THE BLACK HILLS!" There was gold, lots of it. Best of all, it was easy to find.

The rush was on! Even though it was forbidden by the Treaty of 1868, thousands of white miners hurried to the Black Hills to dig for gold.

Sitting Bull learned about the miners later that year. At the time he was living farther north.

He said, "Friends, what are they talking about? The Black Hills belong to me....I take fresh courage."

Sitting Bull meant that he would stand up to the Americans if they invaded the Black Hills.

In November 1875, President Grant made a decision. All Native Americans must move to the Great Sioux Reservation whether or not they signed the treaty. At the time, there were about 3,400

When gold was discovered in the Black Hills in 1874, miners from around the country traveled there to try their luck.

Lakota and Cheyenne who did not live on the reservation.

With President Grant's approval, the Secretary of the Interior wrote that all Native Americans had to report to the reservation by January 31, 1876. If they did not, they would "be deemed hostile and treated accordingly by the military force."

It was winter, and the bands had scattered across the Plains. It was impossible for messengers to reach them and tell them about the orders from Washington, D.C. Even if they had learned of the orders, it was too cold and difficult for the Native Americans to move their camps. Many years later, White Bull said, "Maybe, if we had had automobiles, we could have made it."

Sitting Bull's group camped near the Yellowstone River. Most likely, Sitting Bull never heard the orders. If he had, he ignored them. He said he would "die on a good American horse, fighting the whites."

On February 1, 1876, the Americans began their war against Sitting Bull and other "hostile" Native

Americans. General George Crook and General Alfred Terry commanded the soldiers. Their armies would force the Native Americans onto the reservation.

On March 1, 1876, General Crook's soldiers set out to find the Native Americans not living on the reservation. On March 17, they captured and burned Crazy Horse's camp. The survivors fled to Sitting Bull's camp where they were welcomed.

Sitting Bull was angry. He said, "We stand together, or they will rub us out separately. These soldiers have come shooting. They want war. All right, we will give it to them."

Lt. Colonel George Armstrong Custer was eager to fight Sitting Bull again. Colonel Custer served under General Terry. Victory against Sitting Bull would make Custer famous across America. Custer wanted to be president of the United States. He believed defeating the Native Americans would make him so popular that he would be elected.

Sitting Bull wanted the Native Americans to unite and fight. He hoped that when the Americans

After serving as a general in the Civil War, Ulysses S. Grant was elected president of the United States in 1868.

saw so many Native Americans united, they would make peace.

Riders spread the word to the scattered bands. Through April, May, and June the Native American camp grew daily. The Cheyenne were first, followed by the Oglala, the Miniconjou, the Sans Arc, and the Blackfeet. Last were Sitting Bull's Hunkpapa followers.

Every few days the Native Americans moved the camp to find food, firewood, fresh grass, and clean water.

As before, Sitting Bull would not seek a fight first. Many young warriors found this hard to accept. They wanted to count coup and "Ride the Daring Line."

Late that May, Sitting Bull prayed to Wakantanka. He dreamed of a cloud of dust coming from the east. From the west blew a white cloud, which looked like a Lakota village. The two clouds crashed together. Lightning flashed and thunder boomed. When the dust cloud disappeared, the white cloud drifted on.

Sitting Bull explained his dream. The eastern

dust cloud was the white soldiers. The western white cloud was their great Native American village. The two clouds crashing together meant a battle in which the white cloud, the Native Americans, won.

The tribes sent scouts to watch for the soldiers.

A few days later Sitting Bull went to a hilltop. He prayed,

Wakantanka, save me and give me all my wild game animals and have them close enough so my people will have enough food this winter . . . be of good nature so all the Lakota nations get along well. If you do this for me, I will Sun Dance two days and two nights and will give you a whole buffalo.

A dance pole was raised and Sitting Bull leaned against it. Jumping Bull, his adopted brother, took a sharp knife. Starting on Sitting Bull's left arm, he made many small cuts. He did the same on Sitting Bull's right arm. These cuts showed how Sitting Bull gave his blood for his people.

Sitting Bull danced, singing and circling the pole

while gazing at the sun. After many hours, he suddenly stopped. He was lowered to the ground and given water. He explained that he heard a voice and saw a vision. He saw soldiers and horses riding upside down into their camp. This meant the Americans were going to die.

Wakantanka had told Sitting Bull, "These soldiers do not possess ears." This meant they had not listened to Sitting Bull's warning.

Wakantanka continued, "They are to die, but you are not supposed to take their spoils." The Great Spirit did not want the Native Americans to take the soldiers' belongings. Sitting Bull believed if they did so, they would become like white men. He warned his warriors to leave the soldiers' things alone.

The Native Americans celebrated. Sitting Bull's visions meant they would win a great victory over the American soldiers. But no one knew when.

The battle came sooner than anyone expected.

CHAPTER 11

LITTLE BIGHORN

THE AMERICAN ARMY PLANNED TO surround the Native Americans. Then the soldiers would slowly close in.

Meanwhile, more Native Americans joined Sitting Bull.

On June 16, 1876, Sitting Bull's scouts spotted General Crook's army. They raced to camp, shouting the news.

Sitting Bull still would not fight unless attacked first. That night, however, about 500 young warriors rode off to fight the invading Americans. Sitting Bull, realizing he could not stop the battle, galloped to join them. More than 1,000 warriors, including his friend Crazy Horse, rode with him.

By eight o'clock that morning General Crook's men had marched for two hours. The general ordered a stop to rest. Thinking he was safe, he played a game of cards.

Crook trusted his Crow and Shoshoni scouts. These Native Americans had fought the Lakota and the Cheyenne for years. They had joined the American soldiers to get revenge.

The Lakota and the Cheyenne warriors met the Crow and the Shoshoni scouts. They battled while Crook's soldiers caught up. All day the two sides fought along Rosebud Creek.

Sitting Bull's warriors charged, shot, and fell back. The Americans attacked. Back and forth both sides fought and retreated. One Lakota warrior said, "Sometimes we chased them, sometimes they chased us."

Sitting Bull did not fight. His arms were swollen from the Sun Dance cuts. He shouted, "Be brave, boys! Be brave."

At day's end Sitting Bull's warriors pulled back. They had fought all day after riding all night. Twenty warriors died. Twenty more were wounded.

General Crook claimed victory. He said, "The command finally drove the Indians back in great confusion."

Sitting Bull felt he had won. His warriors had stopped an army twice their size.

Four days later, after mourning their dead, Sitting Bull's people held a victory celebration. The dancing, feasting, and singing lasted six days. Warriors proudly shared their battle coups. White Bull, Sitting Bull's nephew, said, "I have lived up to my good name and counted five coups."

Sitting Bull's camp had doubled in size. There were more than 1,000 tipis and 7,000 people. Sitting Bull could count on 1,800 armed warriors in the next battle. He wondered, however, when the upside-down soldiers from his dream would fall into their village.

His camp moved to the Greasy Grass River to find food and water. The Americans called this river Little Bighorn.

Sitting Bull climbed a ridge. He prayed, "Wakantanka, pity me. In the name of the tribe I offer you this peace pipe. Wherever the sun, the moon, the earth, the four points of the wind, there you are always. Father, save the tribe. I beg you. Pity me. We want to live. Guard us against all misfortunes.... Pity me."

Sitting Bull did not know Custer was near. He did not realize the next day would bring the big battle that both the Native Americans and the Americans expected.

Custer was not with General Crook at the earlier battle against Sitting Bull along Rosebud Creek. Custer and the 750 men of the Seventh Cavalry were under the command of General Terry. Now Custer wanted his chance to fight Sitting Bull. He searched for the main Native American village.

Custer's soldiers found the Native Americans' trail on June 22. He followed hoofprints, footprints, and tipi pole marks in search of them.

On June 24, Custer reached the site where Sitting Bull had performed his Sun Dance. There the trail became confused. Hoofprints and footprints were jumbled. Pole marks were blurred.

Custer did not know those marks meant even more Native Americans had joined Sitting Bull.

On June 25, Custer's scouts saw smoke rising from Sitting Bull's village. They saw Sitting Bull's warriors spying on them. Custer decided to fight.

It was hot and dry. Sitting Bull's tired warriors were resting in their tipis. Boys swam and watered the ponies. Girls gathered berries and roots. Women cooked.

Suddenly Sitting Bull's scouts raced in shouting, "They are charging, the chargers are coming!"

Warriors painted themselves for battle. Women packed. Boys rounded up the ponies.

Then American soldiers charged across the Little Bighorn River straight into Sitting Bull's camp!

The Battle of Little Bighorn had begun.

Bullets flew, shredding tipis. Old people sang death songs for the warriors. Mothers grabbed children and ran for safety.

Sitting Bull jumped on a horse and pulled up his

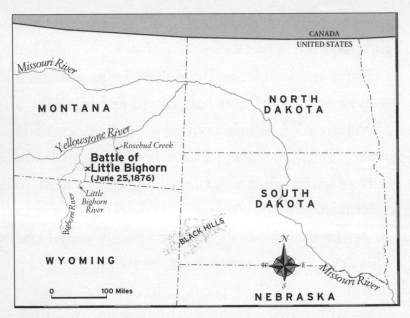

The Battle of Little Bighorn was fought near the Little Bighorn River. It was an important event in the struggle between the American government and the Lakota Sioux.

mother and sister. They galloped to a hilltop. Sitting Bull left them to race back for the rest of his family.

Sitting Bull handed his beloved shield to his adopted son One Bull. One Bull gave Sitting Bull a pistol and rifle.

Sitting Bull was tired from his Sun Dance and the last battle. At first, he did not join the fight. After rescuing his family, he shouted to the warriors, "Brave up! We have everything to fight for. If we're defeated, we'll have nothing to live for. It'll be a hard time, but fight like brave men! Brave up!"

Custer split his soldiers into three groups. The first group, commanded by Captain Frederick Benteen, attacked Sitting Bull's camp. Custer and more than 200 soldiers rode around to attack the camp from a different place. The third group, under the command of Major Marcus Reno, followed behind.

Reno said later, "The very earth seemed to grow Indians."

Outnumbered, the white soldiers were losing.

Custer and about 100 of his soldiers gathered on a ridge top. This place, where Sitting Bull had prayed the night before, would be their last stand.

Crazy Horse, White Bull, and hundreds of warriors attacked the ridge. Custer and his men dug in. They hid behind their dead horses, then rose to fire. The Lakota and the Cheyenne surrounded them. One by one, Custer's men were killed.

White Bull described the battle's last moments

like this: "I charged in. A tall, well-built soldier with yellow hair and mustache [who might have been Custer] saw me coming. We grabbed each other and wrestled there in the dust and smoke. It was like fighting in a fog. . . . That was a fight, a hard fight."

The final part of the Battle of Little Bighorn lasted less than an hour.

Custer and the men who had ridden into battle under his direct command died. Another fifty-three soldiers were killed and sixty more wounded.

No one knows exactly how many Native Americans died. From the Lakota accounts, it was probably fewer than forty.

After the battle, Sitting Bull said, "My heart is full of sorrow that so many were killed on each side, but when they compel [make] us to fight, we must fight. Tonight we shall mourn our dead, and those brave white men lying up yonder on the hillside."

Four days later, after their dead had been honored, the various tribes celebrated their great victory together. They had defeated more soldiers

This pictograph by Amos Bad Heart Bull, an Oglala Sioux, shows Sitting Bull and Crazy Horse riding in front of their warriors at the Battle of Little Bighorn.

than ever before. They hoped the whites would now leave them in peace.

After the celebration, the Native Americans split up. Some returned to the reservation. Others followed Crazy Horse to the Black Hills. Some headed west or north to hunt buffalo.

Sitting Bull and his band rode east to Killdeer Mountain in North Dakota.

Sitting Bull did not know that Little Bighorn would be the Native Americans' last major victory.

Today white stones mark the places were U.S. soldiers died at the Battle of Little Bighorn.

Never before had so many Native Americans united under one leader to fight the Americans. Never again would they do so. It had taken Sitting Bull's skills to bring them together, but once again they were scattered.

Sitting Bull had no idea what was happening back east. On July 4, 1876, America had joyously celebrated its first 100 years. On July 6, the first newspaper accounts of the battle appeared.

The *Bismarck Tribune* headline that day read, "MASSACRED. GEN. CUSTER AND 261 MEN VICTIMS. NO OFFICER OR MAN OF 5 COMPANIES LEFT TO TELL THE TALE." Newspapers around the country repeated the story. Many added their own details, many of which were not true.

The Native Americans were said to be horrible savages. Sitting Bull was said to be the worst.

Sitting Bull could not understand why so many Americans hated him so much. He said, "Is it wrong for me to love my own? Is it wicked for me because my skin is red? Because I am Lakota? Because I was born where my father lived? Because I would die for my people and my country?"

CHAPTER 12

ESCAPE TO CANADA

THE NATIVE AMERICAN VICTORY AT Little Bighorn angered the United States government. Officials decided to end the Native American "problem" once and for all. They would attack the Native Americans until they surrendered or were killed.

General Philip Sheridan was given overall command. He ordered General Crook and General Terry to take away horses and guns from all Native Americans on the reservation.

Next, he sent soldiers to the grazing lands to kill as many buffalo as possible. He knew the Native Americans could not survive without enough buffalo.

Trains that crossed the Plains would sometimes stop to allow passengers time to shoot buffalo for sport.

Since 1850 the number of buffalo had fallen sharply. White hunters killed millions for their hides and tongues. General Sheridan's order had made the situation even worse. Sitting Bull said, "A cold wind blew across the prairie when the last buffalo fell . . . a death wind for my people."

By the end of the summer of 1876, half the U.S. army, 9,000 soldiers, was out west. First General Crook, then Colonel Nelson A. Miles pursued Sitting Bull.

That fall, learning Colonel Miles was near his camp, Sitting Bull had a friend write a note to him.

I want to know what you are doing traveling on this road. You scare all the buffalo away. I want to hunt on the place. I want you to turn back from here. If you don't, I will fight you again. . . . Turn back from here.

I am your friend,

SITTING BULL

Colonel Miles asked Sitting Bull to meet with him. Sitting Bull agreed. He would try once more to make peace with the Americans.

Colonel Miles asked Sitting Bull to surrender his ponies and rifles and bring his people to the reservation. Sitting Bull said no. He told Colonel Miles to take his soldiers and forts away. He wanted to live without being bothered and to hunt where he chose.

After two days of arguing, Colonel Miles said he

would attack the Native Americans if Sitting Bull did not surrender.

The warriors and soldiers faced off. After some fighting, the Native Americans withdrew.

Colonel Miles chased them. The Native Americans split into smaller bands. Sitting Bull and thirty Hunkpapa families went north. The other bands rode west and were captured by Colonel Miles. Sitting Bull escaped.

Winter came and the Hunkpapa suffered. Many surrendered just to get food. Sitting Bull refused.

A few battles were fought. Sitting Bull's camp was captured, but his people fled to safety. Their winter supplies were burned by the Americans.

More starving Native Americans surrendered. The remaining bands scattered to find food. Sitting Bull's uncle Four Horns went north to Canada where he would be safe from Colonel Miles.

Sitting Bull said to his people, "Friends, we can go nowhere without seeing the head of an American. Our land is small, it is like an island in a lake. We have two ways to go now—to the land of the

The Hunkpapa called Canada "Grandmother's Land" after Queen Victoria.

Grandmother [Queen Victoria's Canada], or to the land of the Spaniards [Mexico]."

Reluctantly, Sitting Bull decided to join his uncle. In early May 1877, Sitting Bull crossed into Canada. Under the protection of the "Great White Mother," Queen Victoria, the Americans could not attack him.

The Canadians told Sitting Bull that his people could not cross back into America to raid or hunt. If they did so, they would have to leave Canada forever. Hungry and desperate, Sitting Bull agreed.

There was nothing the Americans could do unless Sitting Bull crossed back over the border. In October 1877, General Terry led a group of Americans to meet Sitting Bull in Fort Walsh, Canada.

Sitting Bull had erected his worn-out tipi outside Fort Walsh. He refused to camp with anyone else. He was mourning his nine-year-old son, who had just died from an illness.

General Terry and Sitting Bull met on October 17. Terry asked Sitting Bull to return to America and surrender. "It is time for the bloodshed to cease," Terry said. He added, "Should you attempt to return with arms in your hands, you must be treated as enemies of the United States."

Sitting Bull said, "You come here to tell us lies, but we don't want to hear them." With a sharp edge to his voice, Sitting Bull added, "Don't you say two more words. Go back home where you came from."

General Terry asked one last question. "Shall we say to the President that you refuse the offers he has made to you?"

Sitting Bull replied, "You think I am a fool, but you are a greater fool than I am. . . . That is all I have to say. You belong on the other side. This side belongs to us."

The Native Americans shook hands with their Canadian friends. They ignored the Americans.

Sitting Bull was determined to live in Canada for the rest of his life.

There were still small buffalo herds in Canada, but each hunt brought fewer animals.

Many starving Native Americans returned to the United States. They surrendered for food. Each year Sitting Bull's band grew smaller. By 1880, fewer than 200 Hunkpapa remained with him.

Sitting Bull refused to surrender. He said, "I will remain what I am until I die, a hunter, and when there are no buffalo or other game I will send my children to hunt and live on prairie mice, for where an Indian is shut up in one place his body becomes weak."

By May 1881, the food for Sitting Bull's band was almost gone. Hunkpapa children were sick and malnourished. Old people were dying. Sitting Bull had to surrender to save them.

One American who witnessed Sitting Bull's surrender wrote, "Nothing but nakedness and starvation has driven this man to submission, and that not on his own account but for the sake of his children, of whom he is very fond."

On July 20, 1881, Sitting Bull surrendered at Fort Buford in present-day North Dakota. His family and followers numbered about 190.

Sitting Bull did not look like the fierce warrior Americans read about. He wore a dirty shirt and leather leggings. He wrapped a torn blanket around his waist. He had an eye infection. His horse stumbled.

Still, Sitting Bull walked with pride.

The Native Americans gave up their rifles and

ponies. Sitting Bull did not hand over his rifle. Instead, he asked his son Crow Foot to surrender it for him.

Sitting Bull said, "I surrender this rifle to you through my young son. I wish it to be remembered that I was the last man of my tribe to surrender my rifle."

He sang his song of defeat:

> *A warrior I have been.*
> *Now, it is all over.*
> *A hard time I have.*

CHAPTER 13

PRISONER
OF WAR

SITTING BULL SURRENDERED HIS RIFLE and pony. He did not surrender his spirit.

The United States feared Sitting Bull might still lead a Lakota uprising. He was put under the army's control. A week later the steamboat *General Sherman* took Sitting Bull and his 190 family members and followers to Bismarck in present-day North Dakota.

He was dressed in an old pair of blue pants, a white shirt, and worn out moccasins. He wore old clothes because he had given his better clothes to those who needed them.

A curious crowd gathered to see this fierce fighter who had defeated Custer. Was this tired, old man really the fierce Sitting Bull they had heard so much about?

Sitting Bull had never been in a town. As a boy he had been called Slow for the way he studied the world. With his steady gaze he studied this new world the same way.

Sitting Bull was offered a train ride. When the train engine moved, Sitting Bull said he would rather walk into town.

In Canada, Sitting Bull had learned to write his name. Someone asked for his autograph. This was the first of many autographs he signed. He never charged children or women, but he made men pay. Generous as always, he often gave his money away to poor children.

A dinner was given for the Native Americans. Sitting Bull marveled at the ice cream served for dessert.

Sitting Bull boarded the steamboat again. They traveled to the Standing Rock Agency on the western bank of the Missouri River in southern North Dakota. The agency, a government post with

While living in Canada, Sitting Bull learned to sign his name. He often signed autographs for children and adults.

offices and warehouses, was part of the Great Sioux Reservation. Guarded by Fort Yates, the Standing Rock Agency was where many Lakota came for their treaty payments of food and supplies.

After three weeks the government decided Sitting Bull was a prisoner of war. He would be sent to Fort Randall near the Nebraska border to be under the army's control.

On September 9, 1881, he was forced aboard a steamboat. Soldiers went along to make sure nothing happened.

At Fort Randall, Sitting Bull was told where to put his tipi and when to come for food. He was not given land or farming tools.

The next twenty months were difficult ones for Sitting Bull. He sometimes met with friends. They talked over past days, bragging about their coups. Sitting Bull listened but rarely spoke.

In his heart he realized his old way of life had ended. Still, he hoped the Americans would let him be free.

Sitting Bull said, "The life my people want is a life

of freedom. I have seen nothing the white man has, houses or railways or clothing or food, that is as good as the right to move in the open country, and live in our own fashion."

Putting his people first, however, Sitting Bull changed. He would make the best of his new life. He would farm, not hunt. He would raise cattle, not chase buffalo. He would live in a cabin, not a tipi. He would dress in cloth, not buffalo leather. His children would go to school to learn the white man's ways.

Patiently, he waited to return to Standing Rock to begin his new way of life.

CHAPTER 14

STANDING ROCK

IN APRIL 1883, SITTING BULL LEFT FORT Randall for Standing Rock. He was no longer a prisoner. At Standing Rock, though, he would be under the control of Major James McLaughlin.

Sitting Bull was still a Hunkpapa chief and holy man. He was determined to guide his people even on the reservation.

He told Major McLaughlin that he, Sitting Bull, was the main chief. McLaughlin told him he might have once been an important chief, but at Standing Rock he would be treated like the other Native Americans.

Sitting Bull now had a new enemy. Over the next seven years, Sitting Bull would struggle with McLaughlin. Sitting Bull would fight for the rights of his people. He would not give in easily to McLaughlin's commands.

McLaughlin knew Sitting Bull was an important leader. He wrote, Sitting Bull "was by far the most influential man of his nation for many years, neither Gall, Spotted Tail, nor Red Cloud [other Sioux chiefs] ... [had] the power that he did."

Sitting Bull was able to choose a quiet place about twenty miles from Fort Yates for his new home. Fifty-three winters earlier he had been born nearby.

A relative gave him a log cabin. Within three years he was growing corn, oats, and potatoes. He had twenty horses, fifty cattle, and a flock of chickens. He sent his children to the reservation school.

One day Sitting Bull saw his friend, the meadowlark. The bird warned him, "Lakotas will kill you." Would his own people really turn against him and kill him? he may have wondered.

Sitting Bull was not always confined to Standing Rock. In 1884, Major McLaughlin took him on a trip to St. Paul, Minnesota.

Posters like this one advertised Buffalo Bill's Wild West show as the tour traveled from city to city.

He visited the state capital, a printing factory, and a bank. He saw huge machines making clothes. He had a pair of shoes made. He even got to pull a fire alarm. For two weeks Sitting Bull was treated like a star, something he enjoyed.

The next year Sitting Bull really became a star. Buffalo Bill Cody admired Sitting Bull and asked him to join his Wild West show that traveled around America.

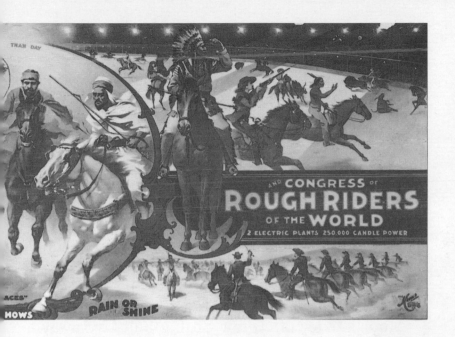

Their first big show was in New York City. Sitting Bull dressed in fine Native American clothes. He and his friends smoked their pipes in front of a tipi set up on stage. While they acted, a narrator told the audience about Native American life on the Plains.

Sitting Bull was a great success. Six thousand people came to the first show to see the "wild Indians."

In 1885, Sitting Bull joined Buffalo Bill's show again. The two had become friends. One advertising poster read, "Foes in '76, Friends in '85." Buffalo Bill liked Sitting Bull so much he gave him his horse from the show. The horse was trained to sit down and raise a hoof into the air when it heard gunfire.

Annie Oakley, the famous sharpshooter who performed in Buffalo Bill's show, was another friend. Sitting Bull admired her shooting skills so much that he called her "Little Sure Shot." He adopted her as a daughter.

Annie Oakley often saw Sitting Bull give away money he earned from selling autographed pictures. She said the money "went into the pockets of small, ragged boys." Sitting Bull could not understand how Americans sometimes ignored the poor.

During his travels, Sitting Bull saw many wonders of the white world. He also saw great poverty and suffering. He felt that "the farther my people keep away from the whites, the better I shall be satisfied."

He said, "I would rather die an Indian than live a white man."

Annie Oakley demonstrated her sharpshooting skills in Buffalo Bill's Wild West show. She would shoot a dime out of her husband's hand as part of her act.

Over the years more and more American settlers moved west. These people wanted Lakota land. The United States decided to buy the land from the Native Americans. The government wrote a treaty dividing the Great Sioux Reservation into six smaller reservations. Millions of acres could then be sold to Americans.

In 1888, the government sent men to convince the Native Americans to sign the treaty. Two-thirds of the adult Native Americans needed to agree.

Sitting Bull refused to sign the treaty. Many others followed him. He said to the Americans, "When I was a boy, the Lakota owned the world. The sun rose and set on their land. They sent ten thousand men to battle. Where are the warriors today? Who slew [killed] them? Where are our lands? Who owns them?" The Americans failed because Sitting Bull would not give up any more land.

Then Sitting Bull was invited to England to meet Queen Victoria. He would not go. "I am needed here," he said. "There is more talk of taking our lands."

He was right. In 1889, the Americans tried again to buy Lakota land. The government raised the price it would pay. They gave feasts and promised friendship with the Native Americans. This time enough Native Americans agreed and signed the treaty. But not Sitting Bull.

In 1890, President Benjamin Harrison signed, too. Now more Lakota lands were open for settlement.

This was a sad time. The Native Americans were no longer free and independent. They depended on the government for food that often arrived late or never came at all. Their lives seemed hopeless. Then, in 1890, word spread about a holy man named Wovoka. He said that if the Native Americans danced his "Ghost Dance" the whites would go away and the buffalo would return.

Many Native Americans believed Wovoka. He offered hope for a better life. All over the West, Native Americans danced the Ghost Dance. Sitting Bull, however, did not. He did encourage his people to dance.

Major McLaughlin was upset with Sitting Bull's attitude. He saw the Ghost Dance as a threat. He felt Sitting Bull was trying to rally his people against the U.S. government.

In December 1890, Sitting Bull decided to go to Pine Ridge Reservation for a Ghost Dance. Pine Ridge was south of Standing Rock.

Major McLaughlin ordered his policemen, called Metal Breasts, to arrest Sitting Bull. The Metal Breasts were Lakota men who were paid by the government.

The Metal Breasts wore blue uniforms with metal badges pinned on their chests. They stopped fights and caught horse thieves. They spied on other Native Americans for the government. Many Metal Breasts were jealous of Sitting Bull's popularity.

Major McLaughlin's orders to his policemen read, "You must not let him [Sitting Bull] escape under any circumstances."

Before dawn on December 15, more than forty Metal Breasts rode to arrest Sitting Bull. They entered his cabin and ordered Sitting Bull to come

This sketch shows several Sioux participating in the Ghost Dance at the Pine Ridge Reservation in South Dakota in December 1890.

with them. After dressing quickly, Sitting Bull stepped out his door.

Two Lakota policemen, Bull Head and Shave Head, held Sitting Bull's arms. They aimed pistols at him. Red Tomahawk, another Metal Breast, walked behind, ready to fire his gun.

Sitting Bull said, "Let me go. I'll go without any assistance."

Friends of Sitting Bull quickly gathered. One of them shouted, "You shall not take our chief."

Catch-The-Bear, another friend, yelled, "You think you are going to take him. You shall not do it."

Sitting Bull then said, "I shall not go."

Bull Head and Shave Head pulled Sitting Bull toward his horse. His friends grew angry and shouted louder.

Suddenly, Catch-The-Bear shot Bull Head. As he fell, Bull Head shot Sitting Bull in the chest. Red Tomahawk shot Sitting Bull in the head.

Sitting Bull fell to the ground, dead.

At the sound of the gunfire, Sitting Bull's horse,

the gift from Buffalo Bill, sat down and raised a hoof just as it had been trained to do.

A battle began between Sitting Bull's friends and the Metal Breasts. Men on both sides died.

The meadowlark had been right. Sitting Bull's own people had killed him.

CHAPTER 15

SITTING BULL
REMEMBERED

AFTER SITTING BULL'S DEATH MANY Lakota went south to the Pine Ridge Reservation. There they hoped to be protected by Chief Red Cloud. Red Cloud had long led the Oglala Lakota against the Americans. He, too, had finally surrendered and lived on a reservation.

Two weeks later the final major battle between the Americans and the Lakota took place.

At Wounded Knee, in present-day South Dakota, a group of Ghost Dancers and their families surrendered to what remained of Custer's Seventh Cavalry under the command of Colonel George A. Forsyth. The winter weather was bitter. The Native Americans were hungry and tired. Their leader, Big Foot, was sick. He thought surrender would be best.

On December 28, 1890, close to 400 Lakotas surrendered. Only 106 of the Native Americans were warriors. The rest were women, children, and the elderly. The American soldiers numbered more than 500.

The Native Americans were ordered to give up their guns. A few old rifles were turned in. The Americans believed there were more guns in Big Foot's camp. Colonel Forsyth ordered the camp to be searched.

A few rifles were found in the tipis. Then Forsyth told his men to search each warrior. He thought they had guns under the blankets they wore. Apparently Black Coyote did have a hidden gun. He took out his rifle and fired into the air. Then a battle erupted with both sides shooting at once.

The American soldiers also shot cannons at the camp. Cannon shells exploded, shredding the tipis. Warriors, women, and children fell wounded or dying. Those not wounded fled. Many ran down into a ravine where they thought they would be safe. Instead, the American soldiers fired on them.

Black Elk, a Lakota warrior and holy man, said later, "Dead women and children and little babies were scattered all along there, where they had been trying to run away." He added, "When I saw this I wished I had died, too, but I was not sorry for the women and children. It was better for them to be happy in the other world, and I wanted to be there, too."

By the end of the day, Colonel Forsyth counted 25 soldiers dead and 39 wounded. The Lakota counted 226 dead.

Following this massacre at Wounded Knee, the lives of the Lakota became more and more difficult. They never received the payments the government owed them for their lands. Jobs were scarce. Many were hungry and lived in poor housing. They had little health care or education.

But the Lakota have a saying, "We shall live again." Inspired by Sitting Bull's wisdom and leadership, they did not give up. Today more than 100,000 Lakota live on and off reservations. Many Lakota now go to college to become teachers, doctors, lawyers, nurses, and computer programmers. Others raise cattle where their ancestors hunted buffalo.

Many of the Lakota traditions that Sitting Bull struggled to keep alive have been revived. Frequent meetings, like powwows, bring families and friends together much as the Sun Dances did in Sitting Bull's time. There the Lakota sing, dance, eat, and have riding and dancing contests. They gather to tell stories and remember their past and plan their future.

Today Sitting Bull is remembered in classrooms, homes, museums, and monuments across America. At Standing Rock a plaque marks the spot where he was first buried, and a sign details his life. There, students can go to Sitting Bull Community College. Many study the Lakota language and customs so they can be passed down to the next generation. The college's motto comes from Sitting Bull's

Sitting Bull was originally buried at Standing Rock (above) in 1890. In 1953, Sitting Bull's relatives moved the grave to its current location near Mobridge, South Dakota.

words: "Let us put our minds together to see what we can build for our children."

For many years, Sitting Bull's followers came to his grave at Standing Rock to honor him. However, the grave was often vandalized. In 1953, Sitting Bull's relatives removed his body to a grassy hilltop near Mobridge, South Dakota. It is not far from

Many Caches, where he was born in 1831. There a towering statue of Sitting Bull looks east across the Missouri River toward the rising sun. Beneath the statue lies the body of the most famous Lakota leader and holy man.

The Lakota say, "A people without history is like wind in the buffalo grass." If the past is forgotten, it will blow away just as wind leaves no trail in the grass.

As a leader of his people, Sitting Bull will never be forgotten.

CHRONOLOGY

1831   The boy who grows up to be Sitting Bull is born in
         present-day South Dakota. He is a member of the
         Hunkpapa tribe of the Lakota (Sioux). His parents
         name him Jumping Badger.

1841   Jumping Badger (now called Slow or Hunkesni)
         kills his first buffalo.

1845   Slow fights in his first battle and counts his first
         coup against a Crow warrior. He is given his father's
         name of Sitting Bull.

1850   Sitting Bull joins hunter and warrior societies.

1856   Sitting Bull is wounded in the foot. He limps for
         the rest of his life.

1857   Sitting Bull is now a war chief. He adopts a
         captured boy as his brother.

1868   Treaty of 1868 creates the Great Sioux Indian
         Reservation. Sitting Bull meets with Father De
         Smet to discuss the treaty. He refuses to sign the
         treaty.

Late   Sitting Bull is elected overall chief of the six
  1860s Lakota tribes.

1874   Gold is discovered in the Black Hills. Miners
         rush in.

1876   (June 25) The Battle of Little Bighorn is fought in
         what is now southeastern Montana. Lieutenant
         Colonel George Custer and his American command
         are killed in this major Native American victory.

1877   Sitting Bull and his followers flee to Canada where they are protected from the Americans.

1881   Sitting Bull surrenders at Fort Buford (Dakota Territory). He is made a prisoner of war at Fort Randall.

1883   Sitting Bull settles at Standing Rock Agency.

1885   Sitting Bull travels with Buffalo Bill's Wild West show.

1889   The Great Sioux Reservation is broken into six smaller reservations.

1890   (December 15) Sitting Bull is killed during an attempted arrest.

BIBLIOGRAPHY

Astrov, Margot, editor. *American Indian Prose and Poetry*. New York: Capricorn Books, 1962.

Bierhorst, John, editor. *The Sacred Path: Spells, Prayers and Powerful Songs of the American Indians*. New York: William Morrow, 1983.

Brandon, William. *The American Heritage Book of Indians*. New York: Dell, 1961.

Brown, Dee. *Bury My Heart At Wounded Knee: An Indian History of the American West*. New York: Washington Square Press, 1970.

Campbell, Walter S. His notebooks in Boxes 105 and 106 of the Campbell Collection, University of Oklahoma, Norman, OK.

Cody, William. *Buffalo Bill's Life Story: An Autobiography*. New York: Rinehart and Company, 1947.

Colbert, David, editor. *Eyewitness to America: 500 Years of American History in the Words of Those Who Saw It*. New York: Vintage Books, 1998.

Hunt, Sarah, editor. *The Illustrated Atlas of Native American History*. Edison, NJ: Chartwell Books, 1999.

McHugh, Tom. *The Time of the Buffalo*. New York: Knopf, 1972.

Neihardt, John G. *Black Elk Speaks*. Lincoln, NE: University of Nebraska Press, 1979.

John Neihardt. Papers and audio tapes. University of Missouri, Columbia, MO.

Praus, Alexis. *A New Pictographic Autobiography of Sitting Bull*. Washington, DC: Smithsonian Institution, 1955.

Utley, Robert. *The Lance and The Shield, The Life and Times of Sitting Bull*. New York: Henry Holt, 1993.

Vestal, Stanley. *Sitting Bull, Champion of the Sioux*. Norman, OK: University of Oklahoma Press, 1956.

Yue, David and Charlotte. *The Tipi, A Center of Native American Life*. New York: Knopf, 1984.

FURTHER READING

Benchley, Nathaniel. *Only Earth and Sky Last Forever*. New York: Scholastic, 1972.

Bial, Raymond. *The Sioux*. White Plains, NY: Marshall Cavendish, 1999.

Bodow, Stephen. *Sitting Bull: Sioux Leader*. Austin, TX: Raintree Steck-Vaughn, 1994.

Bruchac, Joseph. *A Boy Called Slow*. New York: The Putnam and Grosset Group, 1994.

Eisenberg, Lisa. *The Story of Sitting Bull: Great Sioux Chief*. New York: Dell Yearling, 1991.

Freedman, Russell. *Buffalo Hunt*. New York: Holiday House, 1988.

————. *Indian Chiefs*. New York: Holiday House, 1988.

Marrin, Albert. *Sitting Bull and His World*. New York: Dutton Children's Books, 2000.

McGovern, Ann. *If You Lived With The Sioux Indians*. New York: Scholastic, 1994.

Scheichert, Elizabeth. *Sitting Bull: Sioux Leader*. Springfield, NJ: Enslow Publishers, 1997.

FOR MORE INFORMATION

National Buffalo Museum
Jamestown, North Dakota
This new museum highlights the role that the buffalo played in American history. Interesting and informative exhibits display the life cycle of the buffalo, the value to Native Americans, the hunting of the buffalo almost to extinction, and its recovery today. The museum also has a small roaming herd of buffalo for viewers to enjoy. A restored pioneer village is next door.

(P.O. Box 1712, Jamestown, ND 58402)
(701) 252-8648

North Dakota Heritage Center
Bismarck, North Dakota
This extensive museum traces North Dakota history from prehistoric days to today. Numerous exhibits display aspects of Native American life from buffalo hunting dioramas to the first marker of Sitting Bull's grave. In addition to the Native American exhibits, there are sections devoted to railroads and pioneers—both of which influenced Sitting Bull's life.

(612 East Boulevard Avenue, Bismarck, ND 58505-0830)

(701) 328-2666

Web site: www.state.nd.us/hist

North Dakota Tourism Web Site
This Web site has information about the history of the Great Plains. Discover more about Sitting Bull, Crazy Horse, George A. Custer, Lewis and Clark, and buffalo.

Web site: www.ndtourism.com

PHOTO CREDITS

Photo N20142 from the National Museum of the American Indian (Suitland, MD): 7; Smithsonian Institution National Anthropological Archives (Washington, D.C.): 9, 29; North Wind Pictures Archive (Alfred, ME): 13, 16, 19, 24, 40, 43, 47, 54, 86, 89, 92; Library of Congress (Washington, D.C.): 35, 58, 66, 99, 104–105, 111; National Archives (Washington, D.C.): 60; Seaver Center for Western History Research, Los Angeles County Museum of Natural History (Los Angeles, CA): 70; AP/Wide World Photos (New York, NY): 73; Scholastic Inc./Jim McMahon (New York, NY): 82; The Granger Collection (New York, NY): 85; Richard K. Fox, 1889: 107; Western History Collection, Denver Public Library (Denver, CO): 118

INDEX

Bold numbers refer to photographs

ABOUT THE AUTHORS

Since 1980, Peter and Connie Roop have written sixty fiction and nonfiction books for young readers. They have written biographies, nature books and historical fiction, and they have edited the actual journals of the Pilgrims, Lewis and Clark, and Columbus.

The Roops enjoy writing the stories they find in history. Through research and imagination, they have experienced a Blackfeet buffalo jump in Montana and sailed with Columbus. They have followed the footsteps of Benjamin Franklin in Philadelphia and spied for George Washington. They have kept lighthouse lights burning and searched for whales. Through learning about history, the Roops hope to share the stories of people who lived long ago with the readers of today.

Connie teaches high-school environmental science. At her school, she has grown a prairie and dug a wetland. Peter, now a full-time author and speaker, taught elementary school for twenty-five years. He was named Wisconsin State Teacher of the Year in 1987.

When not writing or teaching, the Roops travel with their children, Heidi and Sterling. Their goal as a family is to travel to all seven continents together. So far, they have visited South America, North America, and Europe. Africa is next!